WORLD'S GREATEST CELEBRATIONS

HOLI

Michelle Lee

World's Greatest Celebrations: Holi

Scobre Educational
42982 Osgood Road
Fremont, CA 94539

www.scobre.com
info@scobre.com

Scobre Educational publications may be purchased for
educational, business, or sales promotional use.

Cover and Layout by Sara Radka
Edited by Lauren Dupuis-Perez
Copyedited by Malia Green
Images sourced from iStock, Shutterstock, Alamy, and Newscom

ISBN: 978-1-62920-573-1 (hardcover)
ISBN: 978-1-62920-572-4 (eBook)

TABLE OF CONTENTS

INTRODUCTION

Holi is a **Hindu** moon festival that is celebrated in India and other places around the world. In the Hindu calendar, Holi begins after the full moon of the month of *Phalunga* (around February to March in the Western calendar). It is a two-day celebration of spring, goodness, love, and colors.

On the night of the full moon, people light bonfires. The bonfires are central to the celebration, as people dance and sing around them. They celebrate the end of winter and the beginning of spring. Many are excited for the new season because it means fruits and vegetables will grow, and the land will be filled with green fields and colorful flowers.

The next day is Holi, and in honor of the colorful spring, people wear old clothes and throw paint at each other on the streets. They carry handfuls of paint or use water guns and balloons to splash each other. The colors are often bright reds, oranges, blues, yellows, and greens. It is a time of letting go and having fun.

DID YOU KNOW?

Hinduism is the third largest religion in the world. They believe in many gods, and that people are reborn after they die. They also believe that all living things—including animals—have a soul, so it is wrong to hurt or kill them.

These paint-throwing games give Holi its name: the Festival of Colors. It is also called the Festival of Love because it brings people together. Friends, family, and strangers throw colors at each other. With the paint on, it is hard to tell who's who. Stranger or friend, rich or poor, young or old—it does not matter. Everyone celebrates together.

During Holi, people throw paint at each other. The bright colors represent spring flowers.

HISTORY

Holi is thousands of years old. The celebration was first followed by women who prayed to the full moon for the happiness and health of their families. Over time, the moon festival became a celebration of spring. More people, including men, began to celebrate, and Holi became a bigger event with more practices and beliefs.

In the 16th century, Indian princes and princesses celebrated by letting go and having fun. They would play with their servants and throw paint at each other while music played in the background. In the 17th century, royal families had more fancy celebrations, which included the king giving gifts to his people and having grand dances. Now, Holi is a mix of all these things. It is celebrated with merrymaking, paint-throwing, singing, dancing, and gift-giving. Holi is also a time to honor Hindu legends and stories.

DID YOU KNOW?

Vishnu is the most important Hindu god. He keeps the world safe and guides people on their journey through life. He has four heads and arms and wears a special stone around his neck. Sometimes Vishnu has different forms. He is also known as the god Krishna.

In Hindu belief, Holi began with the legend of Prince Prahalad and Holika. There once was a king who was very selfish and proud of himself. He wanted his people to **worship** him as a god, including his son Prahalad. Prahalad knew his father was not a god and thought it was wrong to worship him. The prince was very religious and believed strongly in the god **Vishnu**.

During the Holi festival, people burn figures of Holika, a wicked sorceress

Angered, the king ordered his son to be killed. The guards tried to kill Prahalad, but he was protected by Vishnu each time. He survived being thrown into a pit of poisonous snakes and being trampled upon by elephants.

The king could not kill Prahalad, so the king asked his wicked sister, Holika, for help. Holika had magical powers and could not be burned by fire. She carried the boy with her and brought him to the middle of a bonfire. She thought Prahalad would burn while she stayed cool, but the opposite happened. Because Holika used her powers for evil, the gods took away her magic and let her burn, and the good, kind Prahalad survived. The Holi festival takes its name from Holika. It is a celebration of the defeat of evil and a reminder that good always wins.

Krishna and Radha are Hindu gods that are known for the true love between them.

The paint-throwing **tradition** comes from the legend of **Krishna** and Radha. The god Krishna wondered why his skin was dark, since his girlfriend Radha's skin was light. His mother joked and told him he could put paint on Radha and change her to any color he wanted. So he played a prank on Radha and smeared paint all over her face. She responded by throwing paint back at him. This started the fun paint-throwing games Hindus have today. Holi reminds people of the playful side of life as well as the love between Krishna and Radha.

Different parts of India have different stories about Holi. In South India, a popular legend tells the story of the gods **Shiva**, **Parvati**, and **Kamadeva**. Shiva is the Hindu god of darkness. He has three eyes—one of which can blast fire.

The goddess Parvatl was in love with Shiva. She wanted him to fall in love with her and so she asked the god of love, Kamadeva, to shoot one of his love arrows at Shiva. Kamadeva listened to her and attacked Shiva. Shiva became upset and burned Kamadeva to ashes with his third eye.

Parvati is the Hindu goddess of love and power.

Kamadeva's wife cried and pleaded for Shiva to bring her husband back to life. Shiva then understood the love between the two, and granted her wish. Holi remembers this event and celebrates Shiva's act of love and forgiveness. It is a time to forgive the past and fix broken relationships with people. Even enemies are considered friends on this day.

Shiva is also the god of destruction and creation. He represents the natural cycle of life. For example, winter destroys, but spring creates.

Holi brings everyone together as friends.

THE COLORS OF HOLI

Blue represents peace and calm.

Red represents love, warmth, and safety.

Yellow represents happiness.

Green represents health.

Decorating elephants is a Holi tradition in Rajasthan.

Home to more than a billion people, India is the world's second most populated country in the world. Its official languages are Hindi and English, but there are more than 1,000 languages spoken in this region. Many people in India know how to speak more than one language.

Holi is mostly celebrated in the northern part of India. Many states have their own way of celebrating the festival. In the state of Rajasthan, elephants take part in the celebration. They are painted and decorated with beautiful designs. Then people climb onto them and throw paint at each other while riding the elephants. In Punjab, people shout in their loudest voices and display their martial arts skills. There is archery, horse riding, and **fencing**.

Although South India does not celebrate Holi as much as the North, there are still some unique traditions. In Andhra Pradesh, there are graceful gypsy dances. At night, children throw dry colors at each other and ask elders for **blessings** by rubbing paint on their feet.

Many people celebrate Holi with music and dancing.

DID YOU KNOW?

Some English words come from Indian languages. Bandanna comes from the word, *bandha*, meaning "to tie something." Cheetah comes from *chita*, meaning "the spotted one," and *khaki* is an Indian word that means "a gray or dusty color."

MEANING

Holi has many meanings. In most of India, Holi is a happy time because winter is ending. India also becomes more alive and colorful. Flowers are in bloom and plants are green and bright. The paint-throwing tradition is a celebration of these beautiful colors.

In North India, the Hindu legend of Krishna and Radha tells people to have fun once in a while. It also shows people the close, loving relationship between Krishna and Radha and reminds them to be good to their loved ones. Holi is also like Valentine's Day. Sometimes boys and girls show their love to each other.

Boys and girls are loving and kind to each other during the festival.

At night, people light bonfires.

In South India, Holi remembers the story of Shiva and Kamadeva. The bonfires burn in remembrance of Shiva's forgiveness and Kamadeva's new life. The bonfires are also there to keep evil and bad luck away. People are told to let their troubles burn away and to forgive and love one another. Holi is all about celebrating the love between people, the colors of spring, the playfulness and joy of life, as well as Hindu legends and stories.

DID YOU KNOW?

Sometimes people throw dolls that look like Holika into the bonfires. It is to remember that evil is always defeated. The ashes from the bonfires are said to bring good luck.

SPECIAL EVENTS

The celebration of Holi begins at night, during the light of the full moon. People make bonfires on street corners and dance and sing around them. Mothers may also carry their babies around the bonfire in the hopes that good luck will come to their children.

The next morning, Holi is alive with noise and celebration. People run and chase each other. Drums, music, and laughter fill the air. Paint is thrown at everyone, even at strangers and elders. Some places in India celebrate with pretend battles. In Barsana, men carry shields for defense, while women playfully beat them with sticks. The next day, the men get even by charging toward the women and drenching them in red-orange colors. Holi is a day where everyone plays tricks and pranks on each other.

A Holi drummer plays music for the festival.

Holi celebrators clean up at the Ganges River after a morning of paint-throwing and fun.

At noon, most events come to a stop and people go to a river or bath to wash the paint away. Once they are clean and redressed, they visit relatives and exchange gifts.

DID YOU KNOW?

The Barsana tradition comes from another story about Krishna and Radha. Krishna would play pranks on Radha and the other women in the village. They would get back at him by capturing him and making him dance for them. The Barsana tradition remembers Krishna and Radha's playful spirit.

WHAT SETS IT APART

What makes Holi very unique is that it is one of the messiest festivals in the world. People wear their oldest clothes to the paint-throwing games, so no one is worried about ruining their clothes. Children can get messy and have as many colors as they want on their body. It is a special time when everyone relaxes for the day. Children call out and tease each other while some hide and pop out to splash others with colors.

This fun celebration has gained many followers around the world. The United States has its own version called the Color Run. It is an event that combines running with the bright colors of Holi. Runners wear white outfits and get splashed with paint or colored powder for every kilometer they run. Just like the meaning of Holi, the Color Run is all about making everyone happy and bringing the community together. Elsewhere, Holi is celebrated in places like Nepal, South Africa, Bangladesh, Guyana, Mauritius, Pakistan, Surinam, Trinidad and Tobago, and the United Kingdom.

A boy gets ready to throw powder!

The Color Run is an American event that is influenced by Holi.

HIGHLIGHTS

HOLI PAINT

The paint used for Holi comes in two forms: wet or dry. Dry powder is usually made from crushed plants and flowers. When thrown, the powder creates clouds that float in the air for a while. It is very easy to get lost in a mist of colors. Common colors are red, orange, pink, yellow, blue, and green. There are even shiny powders that make the air and people sparkle. To make wet paint, the powders are mixed with water. People use things like bicycle pumps, plastic bottles, water guns, and balloons to splash paint on others.

DID YOU KNOW?

A lot of Holi paint colors come from plants you might see at home. Tomatoes and carrots make red. Marigold and chrysanthemum flowers make yellow. Spinach and mint leaves make green.

DIFFERENCES

Holi is a day about forgetting differences. The festival makes everyone equal because no one judges anyone. People greet strangers in a warm and friendly way—wishing them peace or inviting them to their paint-throwing games. It is hard to see differences because everyone is covered in paint from head to toe. No one can tell who is rich or poor because everyone wears old, worn-out clothing anyway. Holi is also a time for adults to relax and forget about strict rules. Children are not yelled at for getting messy or playing around with others. Even adults act like kids by running, playing, and throwing paint at others.

FOOD

Many Hindus are **vegetarian** and do not eat meat because animals are **sacred** to their religion. There are a lot of delicious vegetarian foods that are eaten during the festival. On the eve of Holi, people roast coconuts over warm bonfires. The next day, people eat *pakora* and *gujiya*. *Pakoras* are crispy, fried vegetables and *gujiya* is a pastry that is shaped like a half moon and filled with milk, fruit, and nuts. Dried fruits and a type of cracker called *mathri* are also favorite snacks. A popular Holi drink is *thandai*—a cool drink made with milk, sugar, almonds, seeds, and herbs.

DID YOU KNOW?

The cow is precious to the Hindu people. Killing cows is not allowed in India and Hindus do not eat any kind of beef.

BOLLYWOOD

Bollywood is the name for the film business in India. It is the Indian version of Hollywood. A lot of Bollywood movies are musicals, and they are famous for capturing the spirit of Indian dance and folk music. Many Bollywood songs are played during Holi. The streets are all alive with people moving and dancing to the same rhythm. Some people play live music with traditional instruments such as the *dohl*. The *dohl* is a big wooden drum people carry in front of them and play with two sticks. Others blast Bollywood music from loudspeakers. Both on and off the screen, Holi is a bright, colorful, and musical party. Visiting Holi will make you feel like you're in a movie.

Surinam

A month before Holi, people plant a castor oil plant called Holika. It is burned on Holi to remember the legend of Prince Prahalad and Holika. Then people celebrate with nightly songs at temples. Rich foods like mango, tamarind, potato balls, and a sweet rice called *kheer* are served.

Gujarat, India

In Gujarat, there is a tradition of breaking pots full of buttermilk. A pot is tied to a rope high above the ground. To reach the pot, groups of people work together to form a human pyramid. The group that succeeds wins a prize while the person who actually breaks the pot is crowned King of Holi.

Basantapur, Nepal
In Nepal, Holi is a week long. A long bamboo pole called *chir* is put up on Basantapur Square. At the top of the *chir*, people hang cloths of many different colors. These are Holi good luck charms. At the end of Holi, the *chir* is burned in a bonfire.

The Color Run, United States
The Color Run is a sports event that was inspired by Holi. The event started as a way to get people to stay active and healthy by making running fun and exciting. It is a five-kilometer race, and people get sprayed with different colors as they pass each kilometer.

THE PEOPLE

In India, millions of people celebrate Holi. It is one of the biggest and liveliest festivals in the country. People parade through the streets—singing and dancing to folk music and popular songs from Bollywood. Others are on rooftops showering the crowds in clouds of paint and color. It is a day to strengthen the bonds of friendship and build a sense of community. Holi is also about being good to loved ones. At the end of the morning activities, people visit their relatives and give them gifts like money, sweets, and new clothes. Children can also play pranks on their family members.

Many famous people also celebrate Holi. Bollywood stars like Kareena Kapoor, Akshay Kumar, and Asin have parties or play with their friends and family. Some even go to the streets and throw colors. With all that paint, it is hard to tell who is a movie star! Some American artists are also influenced by this celebration. In Regina Spektor's music video

for the song "Fidelity" she plays with colored powder and paint and splashes them on black and white walls. In Linkin Park's music video for "The Catalyst," band members throw colored powder at each other.

Bollywood star Kareena Kapoor loves to celebrate Holi.

In Barsana, villagers celebrate Holi by dancing and throwing colors at each other.

IMPACT

Holi and the beauty of India bring millions of visitors to the country each year. According to the Government of India, more than 6 million tourists visited in 2011 and spent about $16 billion at Indian hotels, restaurants, and stores. Every year, this money helps create more jobs and businesses.

Different parts of India have their own way of celebrating Holi. In Barsana, you can watch men and women fight in pretend battles. In Punjab, warriors dress up in fine clothes and jeweled turbans. There are sword fights, martial arts, and even acrobats. Or you can visit New Delhi, the capital of India. They have a Holi festival called "Holi Cow!" Delicious food is sold on the streets, and there are sprinklers to shower people in a sea of colors.

HERE'S A TIP:

Don't try to splash people with paint outside of Holi! If you want to throw some colors, check to see if there are Holi festivals around your neighborhood, or have a party in your own backyard. Just ask your parents first. Also, you can always sign up for the Color Run at thecolorrun.com. They have races throughout the United States, and are even spreading worldwide!

What makes Holi special is that it is celebrated by all and everyone is treated equally. People who do not normally hang out with each other come together. The party is all about forgetting differences and building friendships with the people around you. Children may make new friends while playing paint wars with others on the streets. They can even walk up to strangers and splash them with colors. If the stranger looks shocked or surprised, the children can smile and say "Bura na mano, Holi hai!"

Don't feel offended, it's Holi!

GLOSSARY

blessings: good wishes or special favors

Hindu: someone who follows the religion of Hinduism

Kamadeva: the Hindu god of love

Krishna: a Hindu god who likes to play tricks on people

musical: a play or movie with scenes where the characters sing songs

Parvati: a Hindu goddess and mother of the universe; she later becomes Shiva's wife

sacred: something precious, usually for religious reasons

Shiva: the Hindu god of darkness

soul: a person's spirit or life force

tradition: a set of beliefs and practices that are passed down from generation to generation

turban: a hat or headdress that is made by wrapping a strip of cloth around the head

vegetarian: someone who does not eat any meat or fish

version: a different form or style; a different point of view

Vishnu: a Hindu god and protector of the world

worship: to honor or love someone like a god